# 2020
# Weekly & Monthly Planner

If found please return to:

Phone:
Email:

Copyright Rocket Studio Planners
email: hirocketstudio@gmail.com

# NOTES

# NOTES

# NOTES

# 2020

## January
| S | M | T | W | T | F | S |
|---|---|---|---|---|---|---|
|   |   |   | 1 | 2 | 3 | 4 |
| 5 | 6 | 7 | 8 | 9 | 10 | 11 |
| 12 | 13 | 14 | 15 | 16 | 17 | 18 |
| 19 | 20 | 21 | 22 | 23 | 24 | 25 |
| 26 | 27 | 28 | 29 | 30 | 31 |   |

## February
| S | M | T | W | T | F | S |
|---|---|---|---|---|---|---|
|   |   |   |   |   |   | 1 |
| 2 | 3 | 4 | 5 | 6 | 7 | 8 |
| 9 | 10 | 11 | 12 | 13 | 14 | 15 |
| 16 | 17 | 18 | 19 | 20 | 21 | 22 |
| 23 | 24 | 25 | 26 | 27 | 28 | 29 |

## March
| S | M | T | W | T | F | S |
|---|---|---|---|---|---|---|
| 1 | 2 | 3 | 4 | 5 | 6 | 7 |
| 8 | 9 | 10 | 11 | 12 | 13 | 14 |
| 15 | 16 | 17 | 18 | 19 | 20 | 21 |
| 22 | 23 | 24 | 25 | 26 | 27 | 28 |
| 29 | 30 | 31 |   |   |   |   |

## April
| S | M | T | W | T | F | S |
|---|---|---|---|---|---|---|
|   |   |   | 1 | 2 | 3 | 4 |
| 5 | 6 | 7 | 8 | 9 | 10 | 11 |
| 12 | 13 | 14 | 15 | 16 | 17 | 18 |
| 19 | 20 | 21 | 22 | 23 | 24 | 25 |
| 26 | 27 | 28 | 29 | 30 |   |   |

## May
| S | M | T | W | T | F | S |
|---|---|---|---|---|---|---|
|   |   |   |   |   | 1 | 2 |
| 3 | 4 | 5 | 6 | 7 | 8 | 9 |
| 10 | 11 | 12 | 13 | 14 | 15 | 16 |
| 17 | 18 | 19 | 20 | 21 | 22 | 23 |
| 24 | 25 | 26 | 27 | 28 | 29 | 30 |
| 31 |   |   |   |   |   |   |

## June
| S | M | T | W | T | F | S |
|---|---|---|---|---|---|---|
|   | 1 | 2 | 3 | 4 | 5 | 6 |
| 7 | 8 | 9 | 10 | 11 | 12 | 13 |
| 14 | 15 | 16 | 17 | 18 | 19 | 20 |
| 21 | 22 | 23 | 24 | 25 | 26 | 27 |
| 28 | 29 | 30 |   |   |   |   |

## July
| S | M | T | W | T | F | S |
|---|---|---|---|---|---|---|
|   |   |   | 1 | 2 | 3 | 4 |
| 5 | 6 | 7 | 8 | 9 | 10 | 11 |
| 12 | 13 | 14 | 15 | 16 | 17 | 18 |
| 19 | 20 | 21 | 22 | 23 | 24 | 25 |
| 26 | 27 | 28 | 29 | 30 | 31 |   |

## August
| S | M | T | W | T | F | S |
|---|---|---|---|---|---|---|
|   |   |   |   |   |   | 1 |
| 2 | 3 | 4 | 5 | 6 | 7 | 8 |
| 9 | 10 | 11 | 12 | 13 | 14 | 15 |
| 16 | 17 | 18 | 19 | 20 | 21 | 22 |
| 23 | 24 | 25 | 26 | 27 | 28 | 29 |
| 30 | 31 |   |   |   |   |   |

## September
| S | M | T | W | T | F | S |
|---|---|---|---|---|---|---|
|   |   | 1 | 2 | 3 | 4 | 5 |
| 6 | 7 | 8 | 9 | 10 | 11 | 12 |
| 13 | 14 | 15 | 16 | 17 | 18 | 19 |
| 20 | 21 | 22 | 23 | 24 | 25 | 26 |
| 27 | 28 | 29 | 30 |   |   |   |

## October
| S | M | T | W | T | F | S |
|---|---|---|---|---|---|---|
|   |   |   |   | 1 | 2 | 3 |
| 4 | 5 | 6 | 7 | 8 | 9 | 10 |
| 11 | 12 | 13 | 14 | 15 | 16 | 17 |
| 18 | 19 | 20 | 21 | 22 | 23 | 24 |
| 25 | 26 | 27 | 28 | 29 | 30 | 31 |

## November
| S | M | T | W | T | F | S |
|---|---|---|---|---|---|---|
| 1 | 2 | 3 | 4 | 5 | 6 | 7 |
| 8 | 9 | 10 | 11 | 12 | 13 | 14 |
| 15 | 16 | 17 | 18 | 19 | 20 | 21 |
| 22 | 23 | 24 | 25 | 26 | 27 | 28 |
| 29 | 30 |   |   |   |   |   |

## December
| S | M | T | W | T | F | S |
|---|---|---|---|---|---|---|
|   |   | 1 | 2 | 3 | 4 | 5 |
| 6 | 7 | 8 | 9 | 10 | 11 | 12 |
| 13 | 14 | 15 | 16 | 17 | 18 | 19 |
| 20 | 21 | 22 | 23 | 24 | 25 | 26 |
| 27 | 28 | 29 | 30 | 31 |   |   |

# January

| SUNDAY | MONDAY | TUESDAY | WEDNESDAY |
|---|---|---|---|
|  |  |  | 1<br><br>New Year's Day |
| 5 | 6 | 7 | 8 |
| 12<br><br>*National Kiss a Ginger Day* | 13 | 14 | 15 |
| 19 | 20<br><br>Martin Luther King Day - USA | 21 | 22 |
| 26 | 27 | 28 | 29 |

# 2020

| THURSDAY | FRIDAY | SATURDAY | TOP PRIORITIES |
|---|---|---|---|
| 2 | 3 | 4 | 1.<br><br>2.<br><br>3. |
| 9 | 10 | 11 | **TO DO**<br>☐<br>☐<br>☐ |
| 16 | 17 | 18 | ☐<br>☐<br>☐<br>☐ |
| 23 | 24 | 25 | **NOTES** |
| 30<br><br>*National Croissant Day* | 31 | | |

# February

| SUNDAY | MONDAY | TUESDAY | WEDNESDAY |
|--------|--------|---------|-----------|
|        |        |         |           |
| 2      | 3      | 4       | 5         |
| 9      | 10     | 11      | 12        |
| 16     | 17 <br><br> Presidents Day - USA | 18 | 19 |
| 23     | 24     | 25      | 26        |

# 2020

| THURSDAY | FRIDAY | SATURDAY | TOP PRIORITIES |
|---|---|---|---|
|  |  | 1 | 1. <br><br> 2. <br><br> 3. |
| 6 | 7 | 8 | **TO DO** |
|  | *National Wear Red Day* |  | ☐ <br> ☐ <br> ☐ |
| 13 | 14 | 15 | ☐ <br> ☐ <br> ☐ <br> ☐ |
|  | *Valentines Day* |  |  |
| 20 | 21 | 22 | **NOTES** |
|  |  | *National Margarita Day* |  |
| 27 | 28 | 29 |  |

# March

| SUNDAY | MONDAY | TUESDAY | WEDNESDAY |
|---|---|---|---|
| 1 | 2 | 3 | 4 |
| 8 *International Women's Day* | 9 | 10 | 11 |
| 15 | 16 | 17 *St Patrick's Day* | 18 |
| 22 *Mothers Day - UK* | 23 | 24 | 25 |
| 29 | 30 | 31 | |

# 2020

| THURSDAY | FRIDAY | SATURDAY |
|---|---|---|
| 5 | 6 *National Dress in Blue Day* | 7 |
| 12 | 13 | 14 |
| 19 | 20 | 21 |
| 26 | 27 | 28 |

### TOP PRIORITIES
1.
2.
3.

### TO DO
- ☐
- ☐
- ☐
- ☐
- ☐
- ☐
- ☐

### NOTES

# April

| SUNDAY | MONDAY | TUESDAY | WEDNESDAY |
|---|---|---|---|
|  |  |  | 1 *April Fools Day* |
| 5 | 6 | 7 *National Beer Day* | 8 |
| 12 *Easter Sunday* | 13 *Easter Monday - UK* | 14 | 15 |
| 19 | 20 | 21 | 22 *National Earth Day* |
| 26 | 27 | 28 | 29 |

# 2020

| THURSDAY | FRIDAY | SATURDAY | TOP PRIORITIES |
|---|---|---|---|
| 2 | 3 | 4 | 1. <br> 2. <br> 3. |
| 9 <br> *National Unicorn Day* | 10 <br> Good Friday - UK | 11 | **TO DO** <br> ☐ <br> ☐ <br> ☐ |
| 16 | 17 | 18 | ☐ <br> ☐ <br> ☐ <br> ☐ |
| 23 | 24 | 25 | **NOTES** |
| 30 | | | |

# May

| SUNDAY | MONDAY | TUESDAY | WEDNESDAY |
|---|---|---|---|
| 31 | | | |
| 3 | 4 *National Star Wars Day* | 5 *Cinco de Mayo* | 6 |
| 10 *Mother's Day - USA* | 11 | 12 | 13 |
| 17 | 18 | 19 | 20 |
| 24 | 25 *Late May Bank Holiday - UK Memorial Day - USA* | 26 | 27 |

# 2020

| THURSDAY | FRIDAY | SATURDAY | TOP PRIORITIES |
|---|---|---|---|
|  | 1 | 2 | 1. |
|  |  |  | 2. |
|  |  | *National Fitness Day* | 3. |
| 7 | 8 | 9 | **TO DO** |
|  |  |  | ☐ |
|  |  |  | ☐ |
|  | May Day - UK |  | ☐ |
| 14 | 15 | 16 | ☐ |
|  |  |  | ☐ |
|  |  |  | ☐ |
|  |  |  | ☐ |
| 21 | 22 | 23 | **NOTES** |
| 28 | 29 | 30 |  |

# June

| SUNDAY | MONDAY | TUESDAY | WEDNESDAY |
|---|---|---|---|
|  | 1 *National Go Barefoot Day* | 2 | 3 |
| 7 | 8 | 9 | 10 |
| 14 | 15 | 16 | 17 |
| 21 *Father's Day - USA + UK* | 22 | 23 *National Pink Day* | 24 |
| 28 | 29 | 30 |  |

# 2020

| THURSDAY | FRIDAY | SATURDAY |
|---|---|---|
| 4 | 5<br><br>*National Doughnut Day* | 6 |
| 11 | 12 | 13 |
| 18 | 19 | 20 |
| 25 | 26 | 27 |

## TOP PRIORITIES

1.

2.

3.

## TO DO

☐

☐

☐

☐

☐

☐

☐

## NOTES

# July

| SUNDAY | MONDAY | TUESDAY | WEDNESDAY |
|---|---|---|---|
|  |  |  | 1 |
| 5 *National Hawaii Day* | 6 | 7 | 8 |
| 12 | 13 | 14 | 15 |
| 19 *National Ice Cream Day* | 20 | 21 | 22 |
| 26 *National Aunt & Uncle's Day* | 27 | 28 | 29 |

# 2020

| THURSDAY | FRIDAY | SATURDAY | TOP PRIORITIES |
|---|---|---|---|
| 2 | 3<br><br>Independence Day - USA | 4 | 1.<br><br>2.<br><br>3. |
| 9 | 10 | 11 | **TO DO**<br>☐<br>☐<br>☐ |
| 16 | 17<br><br>*World Emoji Day* | 18 | ☐<br>☐<br>☐<br>☐ |
| 23 | 24 | 25 | **NOTES** |
| 30 | 31 | | |

# August

| SUNDAY | MONDAY | TUESDAY | WEDNESDAY |
|---|---|---|---|
| 30 *National Toasted Marshmellow Day* | 31 August Bank Holiday - UK | | |
| 2 | 3 | 4 | 5 *National Underwear Day* |
| 9 | 10 | 11 | 12 |
| 16 *National Tell a Joke Day* | 17 | 18 | 19 |
| 23 | 24 | 25 | 26 |

# 2020

| THURSDAY | FRIDAY | SATURDAY | TOP PRIORITIES |
|---|---|---|---|
|  |  | 1<br><br>*National Girlfriends Day* | 1.<br><br>2.<br><br>3. |
| 6 | 7 | 8 | **TO DO**<br><br>☐<br>☐<br>☐ |
| 13 | 14 | 15 | ☐<br>☐<br>☐<br>☐ |
| 20 | 21 | 22 | **NOTES** |
| 27 | 28 | 29 |  |

# September

| SUNDAY | MONDAY | TUESDAY | WEDNESDAY |
|---|---|---|---|
|  |  | 1 | 2 |
| 6 | 7 *Labor Day - USA* | 8 | 9 |
| 13 *National Blame Someone Else Day* | 14 | 15 | 16 |
| 20 | 21 | 22 | 23 |
| 27 | 28 | 29 *National Coffee Day* | 30 |

# 2020

| THURSDAY | FRIDAY | SATURDAY | TOP PRIORITIES |
|---|---|---|---|
| 3 | 4 | 5<br><br>*National Cheese Pizza Day* | 1.<br><br>2.<br><br>3. |
| 10 | 11<br><br>*National Make Your Bed Day* | 12 | **TO DO**<br><br>☐<br>☐<br>☐ |
| 17 | 18 | 19 | ☐<br>☐<br>☐<br>☐ |
| 24 | 25 | 26 | **NOTES** |

# October

| SUNDAY | MONDAY | TUESDAY | WEDNESDAY |
|---|---|---|---|
|  |  |  |  |
| 4 *National Taco Day* | 5 | 6 | 7 |
| 11 | 12 Columbus Day - USA | 13 | 14 |
| 18 | 19 | 20 | 21 |
| 25 | 26 | 27 | 28 *National Chocolate Day* |

# 2020

| THURSDAY | FRIDAY | SATURDAY |
|---|---|---|
| 1 | 2 | 3 *National Boyfriend Day* |
| 8 | 9 | 10 |
| 15 *National I Love Lucy Day* | 16 | 17 |
| 22 | 23 | 24 |
| 29 | 30 | 31 *Halloween* |

## TOP PRIORITIES

1.
2.
3.

## TO DO

- ☐
- ☐
- ☐
- ☐
- ☐
- ☐
- ☐

## NOTES

| SUNDAY | MONDAY | TUESDAY | WEDNESDAY |
|---|---|---|---|
| 1 | 2 | 3 | 4 |
| 8 | 9 | 10 | 11 <br><br> Veterans Day - USA |
| 15 | 16 | 17 | 18 <br><br> *National Princess Day* |
| 22 | 23 | 24 | 25 |
| 29 | 30 | | |

# 2020

| THURSDAY | FRIDAY | SATURDAY | TOP PRIORITIES |
|---|---|---|---|
| 5 | 6 | 7 | 1. <br><br>2. <br><br>3. |
| 12 | 13 <br><br> *World Kindness Day* | 14 | **TO DO** <br> ☐ <br> ☐ <br> ☐ |
| 19 | 20 | 21 | ☐ <br> ☐ <br> ☐ <br> ☐ |
| 26 <br><br> Thanksgiving - USA | 27 | 28 | **NOTES** |

# December

| SUNDAY | MONDAY | TUESDAY | WEDNESDAY |
|---|---|---|---|
|  |  | 1 | 2 |
| 6 | 7 | 8 *Pretend To Be A Time Traveller Day* | 9 |
| 13 | 14 | 15 | 16 |
| 20 | 21 | 22 | 23 |
| 27 Boxing Day Holiday - UK | 28 | 29 | 30 *Bacon Day* |

# 2020

| THURSDAY | FRIDAY | SATURDAY | TOP PRIORITIES |
|---|---|---|---|
| 3 | 4 | 5 *International Ninja Day* | 1.<br>2.<br>3. |
| 10 | 11 | 12 | **TO DO**<br>☐<br>☐<br>☐ |
| 17 | 18 *National Ugly Christmas Sweater Day* | 19 | ☐<br>☐<br>☐<br>☐ |
| 24 *Christmas Eve* | 25 Christmas Day | 26 *Boxing Day - UK* | **NOTES** |
| 31 *New Year's Eve* | | | |

# January

**29 SUNDAY**

**30 MONDAY**

**31 TUESDAY**

**1 WEDNESDAY**

**2 THURSDAY**

# 2020

**3    FRIDAY**

**4    SATURDAY**

| TO DO |
|---|
| ☐ |
| ☐ |
| ☐ |
| ☐ |
| ☐ |
| ☐ |
| ☐ |
| ☐ |
| ☐ |
| ☐ |
| ☐ |
| ☐ |
| ☐ |
| ☐ |
| ☐ |
| ☐ |
| ☐ |

# January

**5**    SUNDAY

**6**    MONDAY

**7**    TUESDAY

**8**    WEDNESDAY

**9**    THURSDAY

# 2020

**10 FRIDAY**

**11 SATURDAY**

| | TO DO |
|---|---|
| ☐ | |
| ☐ | |
| ☐ | |
| ☐ | |
| ☐ | |
| ☐ | |
| ☐ | |
| ☐ | |
| ☐ | |
| ☐ | |
| ☐ | |
| ☐ | |
| ☐ | |
| ☐ | |
| ☐ | |
| ☐ | |
| ☐ | |

# January

**12** SUNDAY

**13** MONDAY

**14** TUESDAY

**15** WEDNESDAY

**16** THURSDAY

# 2020

**17   FRIDAY**

**18   SATURDAY**

| | TO DO |
|---|---|
| | ☐ |
| | ☐ |
| | ☐ |
| | ☐ |
| | ☐ |
| | ☐ |
| | ☐ |
| | ☐ |
| | ☐ |
| | ☐ |
| | ☐ |
| | ☐ |
| | ☐ |
| | ☐ |
| | ☐ |
| | ☐ |
| | ☐ |

# January

**19  SUNDAY**

**20  MONDAY**

**21  TUESDAY**

**22  WEDNESDAY**

**23  THURSDAY**

# 2020

**24 FRIDAY**

**25 SATURDAY**

| | TO DO |
|---|---|
| ☐ | |
| ☐ | |
| ☐ | |
| ☐ | |
| ☐ | |
| ☐ | |
| ☐ | |
| ☐ | |
| ☐ | |
| ☐ | |
| ☐ | |
| ☐ | |
| ☐ | |
| ☐ | |
| ☐ | |
| ☐ | |
| ☐ | |

# January/February

**26** SUNDAY

**27** MONDAY

**28** TUESDAY

**29** WEDNESDAY

**30** THURSDAY

# 2020

**31 FRIDAY**

**1 SATURDAY**

| | TO DO |
|---|---|
| ☐ | |
| ☐ | |
| ☐ | |
| ☐ | |
| ☐ | |
| ☐ | |
| ☐ | |
| ☐ | |
| ☐ | |
| ☐ | |
| ☐ | |
| ☐ | |
| ☐ | |
| ☐ | |
| ☐ | |
| ☐ | |
| ☐ | |

# February

**2 SUNDAY**

**3 MONDAY**

**4 TUESDAY**

**5 WEDNESDAY**

**6 THURSDAY**

# 2020

**7 FRIDAY**

**8 SATURDAY**

| TO DO |
|---|
| ☐ |
| ☐ |
| ☐ |
| ☐ |
| ☐ |
| ☐ |
| ☐ |
| ☐ |
| ☐ |
| ☐ |
| ☐ |
| ☐ |
| ☐ |
| ☐ |
| ☐ |
| ☐ |
| ☐ |
| ☐ |

# February

**9 SUNDAY**

**10 MONDAY**

**11 TUESDAY**

**12 WEDNESDAY**

**13 THURSDAY**

# 2020

**14 FRIDAY**

**15 SATURDAY**

| | TO DO |
|---|---|
| | ☐ |
| | ☐ |
| | ☐ |
| | ☐ |
| | ☐ |
| | ☐ |
| | ☐ |
| | ☐ |
| | ☐ |
| | ☐ |
| | ☐ |
| | ☐ |
| | ☐ |
| | ☐ |
| | ☐ |
| | ☐ |
| | ☐ |

# February

**16 SUNDAY**

**17 MONDAY**

**18 TUESDAY**

**19 WEDNESDAY**

**20 THURSDAY**

# 2020

**21 FRIDAY**

**22 SATURDAY**

| TO DO |
|---|
| ☐ |
| ☐ |
| ☐ |
| ☐ |
| ☐ |
| ☐ |
| ☐ |
| ☐ |
| ☐ |
| ☐ |
| ☐ |
| ☐ |
| ☐ |
| ☐ |
| ☐ |
| ☐ |
| ☐ |

# February

**23 SUNDAY**

**24 MONDAY**

**25 TUESDAY**

**26 WEDNESDAY**

**27 THURSDAY**

# 2020

**28 FRIDAY**

**29 SATURDAY**

| TO DO |
|---|
| ☐ |
| ☐ |
| ☐ |
| ☐ |
| ☐ |
| ☐ |
| ☐ |
| ☐ |
| ☐ |
| ☐ |
| ☐ |
| ☐ |
| ☐ |
| ☐ |
| ☐ |
| ☐ |
| ☐ |

# March

1 SUNDAY

2 MONDAY

3 TUESDAY

4 WEDNESDAY

5 THURSDAY

# 2020

**6   FRIDAY**

**7   SATURDAY**

| | TO DO |
|---|---|
| | ☐ |
| | ☐ |
| | ☐ |
| | ☐ |
| | ☐ |
| | ☐ |
| | ☐ |
| | ☐ |
| | ☐ |
| | ☐ |
| | ☐ |
| | ☐ |
| | ☐ |
| | ☐ |
| | ☐ |
| | ☐ |
| | ☐ |

# March

**8** SUNDAY

**9** MONDAY

**10** TUESDAY

**11** WEDNESDAY

**12** THURSDAY

# 2020

**13  FRIDAY**

**14  SATURDAY**

## TO DO

- [ ]
- [ ]
- [ ]
- [ ]
- [ ]
- [ ]
- [ ]
- [ ]
- [ ]
- [ ]
- [ ]
- [ ]
- [ ]
- [ ]
- [ ]
- [ ]
- [ ]

# March

**15** SUNDAY

**16** MONDAY

**17** TUESDAY

**18** WEDNESDAY

**19** THURSDAY

# 2020

**20 FRIDAY**

**21 SATURDAY**

| | TO DO |
|---|---|
| | ☐ |
| | ☐ |
| | ☐ |
| | ☐ |
| | ☐ |
| | ☐ |
| | ☐ |
| | ☐ |
| | ☐ |
| | ☐ |
| | ☐ |
| | ☐ |
| | ☐ |
| | ☐ |
| | ☐ |
| | ☐ |
| | ☐ |

# March

**22** SUNDAY

**23** MONDAY

**24** TUESDAY

**25** WEDNESDAY

**26** THURSDAY

# 2020

**27 FRIDAY**

**28 SATURDAY**

| TO DO |
|---|
| ☐ |
| ☐ |
| ☐ |
| ☐ |
| ☐ |
| ☐ |
| ☐ |
| ☐ |
| ☐ |
| ☐ |
| ☐ |
| ☐ |
| ☐ |
| ☐ |
| ☐ |
| ☐ |
| ☐ |

# March/April

**29** SUNDAY

**30** MONDAY

**31** TUESDAY

**1** WEDNESDAY

**2** THURSDAY

# 2020

3 FRIDAY

4 SATURDAY

| TO DO |
|---|
| ☐ |
| ☐ |
| ☐ |
| ☐ |
| ☐ |
| ☐ |
| ☐ |
| ☐ |
| ☐ |
| ☐ |
| ☐ |
| ☐ |
| ☐ |
| ☐ |
| ☐ |
| ☐ |
| ☐ |
| ☐ |

| 5 | SUNDAY |
|---|---|

| 6 | MONDAY |
|---|---|

| 7 | TUESDAY |
|---|---|

| 8 | WEDNESDAY |
|---|---|

| 9 | THURSDAY |
|---|---|

# 2020

**10 FRIDAY**

**11 SATURDAY**

| | TO DO |
|---|---|
| | ☐ |
| | ☐ |
| | ☐ |
| | ☐ |
| | ☐ |
| | ☐ |
| | ☐ |
| | ☐ |
| | ☐ |
| | ☐ |
| | ☐ |
| | ☐ |
| | ☐ |
| | ☐ |
| | ☐ |
| | ☐ |
| | ☐ |

12 SUNDAY

13 MONDAY

14 TUESDAY

15 WEDNESDAY

16 THURSDAY

# 2020

**17  FRIDAY**

**18  SATURDAY**

TO DO
- ☐
- ☐
- ☐
- ☐
- ☐
- ☐
- ☐
- ☐
- ☐
- ☐
- ☐
- ☐
- ☐
- ☐
- ☐
- ☐
- ☐

19 SUNDAY

20 MONDAY

21 TUESDAY

22 WEDNESDAY

23 THURSDAY

# 2020

**24  FRIDAY**

**25  SATURDAY**

| TO DO |
|---|
| ☐ |
| ☐ |
| ☐ |
| ☐ |
| ☐ |
| ☐ |
| ☐ |
| ☐ |
| ☐ |
| ☐ |
| ☐ |
| ☐ |
| ☐ |
| ☐ |
| ☐ |
| ☐ |
| ☐ |

# April/May

**26** SUNDAY

**27** MONDAY

**28** TUESDAY

**29** WEDNESDAY

**30** THURSDAY

# 2020

1 FRIDAY

2 SATURDAY

## TO DO

- [ ]
- [ ]
- [ ]
- [ ]
- [ ]
- [ ]
- [ ]
- [ ]
- [ ]
- [ ]
- [ ]
- [ ]
- [ ]
- [ ]
- [ ]
- [ ]
- [ ]

# May

3 SUNDAY

4 MONDAY

5 TUESDAY

6 WEDNESDAY

7 THURSDAY

# 2020

**8  FRIDAY**

**9  SATURDAY**

| TO DO |
|---|
| ☐ |
| ☐ |
| ☐ |
| ☐ |
| ☐ |
| ☐ |
| ☐ |
| ☐ |
| ☐ |
| ☐ |
| ☐ |
| ☐ |
| ☐ |
| ☐ |
| ☐ |
| ☐ |
| ☐ |

# May

**10** SUNDAY

**11** MONDAY

**12** TUESDAY

**13** WEDNESDAY

**14** THURSDAY

# 2020

**15 FRIDAY**

**16 SATURDAY**

## TO DO

- [ ]
- [ ]
- [ ]
- [ ]
- [ ]
- [ ]
- [ ]
- [ ]
- [ ]
- [ ]
- [ ]
- [ ]
- [ ]
- [ ]
- [ ]
- [ ]
- [ ]

17 SUNDAY

18 MONDAY

19 TUESDAY

20 WEDNESDAY

21 THURSDAY

# 2020

**22 FRIDAY**

**23 SATURDAY**

| TO DO |
|---|
| ☐ |
| ☐ |
| ☐ |
| ☐ |
| ☐ |
| ☐ |
| ☐ |
| ☐ |
| ☐ |
| ☐ |
| ☐ |
| ☐ |
| ☐ |
| ☐ |
| ☐ |
| ☐ |
| ☐ |

# May

**24** SUNDAY

**25** MONDAY

**26** TUESDAY

**27** WEDNESDAY

**28** THURSDAY

# 2020

**29 FRIDAY**

**30 SATURDAY**

| TO DO |
|---|
| ☐ |
| ☐ |
| ☐ |
| ☐ |
| ☐ |
| ☐ |
| ☐ |
| ☐ |
| ☐ |
| ☐ |
| ☐ |
| ☐ |
| ☐ |
| ☐ |
| ☐ |
| ☐ |
| ☐ |
| ☐ |

# May/June

**31 SUNDAY**

**1 MONDAY**

**2 TUESDAY**

**3 WEDNESDAY**

**4 THURSDAY**

# 2020

**5　FRIDAY**

**6　SATURDAY**

| TO DO |
|---|
| ☐ |
| ☐ |
| ☐ |
| ☐ |
| ☐ |
| ☐ |
| ☐ |
| ☐ |
| ☐ |
| ☐ |
| ☐ |
| ☐ |
| ☐ |
| ☐ |
| ☐ |
| ☐ |
| ☐ |
| ☐ |

# June

**7** SUNDAY

**8** MONDAY

**9** TUESDAY

**10** WEDNESDAY

**11** THURSDAY

# 2020

**12　FRIDAY**

**13　SATURDAY**

| TO DO |
|---|
| ☐ |
| ☐ |
| ☐ |
| ☐ |
| ☐ |
| ☐ |
| ☐ |
| ☐ |
| ☐ |
| ☐ |
| ☐ |
| ☐ |
| ☐ |
| ☐ |
| ☐ |
| ☐ |
| ☐ |

# June

14 SUNDAY

15 MONDAY

16 TUESDAY

17 WEDNESDAY

18 THURSDAY

# 2020

**19  FRIDAY**

**20  SATURDAY**

| TO DO |
|---|
| ☐ |
| ☐ |
| ☐ |
| ☐ |
| ☐ |
| ☐ |
| ☐ |
| ☐ |
| ☐ |
| ☐ |
| ☐ |
| ☐ |
| ☐ |
| ☐ |
| ☐ |
| ☐ |
| ☐ |

# June

**21** SUNDAY

**22** MONDAY

**23** TUESDAY

**24** WEDNESDAY

**25** THURSDAY

# 2020

**26 FRIDAY**

**27 SATURDAY**

| TO DO |
|---|
| ☐ |
| ☐ |
| ☐ |
| ☐ |
| ☐ |
| ☐ |
| ☐ |
| ☐ |
| ☐ |
| ☐ |
| ☐ |
| ☐ |
| ☐ |
| ☐ |
| ☐ |
| ☐ |
| ☐ |

# June/July

**28** SUNDAY

**29** MONDAY

**30** TUESDAY

**1** WEDNESDAY

**2** THURSDAY

# 2020

3     FRIDAY

4     SATURDAY

| TO DO |
|---|
| ☐ |
| ☐ |
| ☐ |
| ☐ |
| ☐ |
| ☐ |
| ☐ |
| ☐ |
| ☐ |
| ☐ |
| ☐ |
| ☐ |
| ☐ |
| ☐ |
| ☐ |
| ☐ |
| ☐ |

# July

**5** SUNDAY

**6** MONDAY

**7** TUESDAY

**8** WEDNESDAY

**9** THURSDAY

# 2020

**10　FRIDAY**

**11　SATURDAY**

| TO DO |
|---|
| ☐ |
| ☐ |
| ☐ |
| ☐ |
| ☐ |
| ☐ |
| ☐ |
| ☐ |
| ☐ |
| ☐ |
| ☐ |
| ☐ |
| ☐ |
| ☐ |
| ☐ |
| ☐ |
| ☐ |

# July

12 SUNDAY

13 MONDAY

14 TUESDAY

15 WEDNESDAY

16 THURSDAY

# 2020

**17　FRIDAY**

**18　SATURDAY**

| | TO DO |
|---|---|
| ☐ | |
| ☐ | |
| ☐ | |
| ☐ | |
| ☐ | |
| ☐ | |
| ☐ | |
| ☐ | |
| ☐ | |
| ☐ | |
| ☐ | |
| ☐ | |
| ☐ | |
| ☐ | |
| ☐ | |
| ☐ | |
| ☐ | |

# July

19 SUNDAY

20 MONDAY

21 TUESDAY

22 WEDNESDAY

23 THURSDAY

# 2020

**24  FRIDAY**

**25  SATURDAY**

| TO DO |
|---|
| ☐ |
| ☐ |
| ☐ |
| ☐ |
| ☐ |
| ☐ |
| ☐ |
| ☐ |
| ☐ |
| ☐ |
| ☐ |
| ☐ |
| ☐ |
| ☐ |
| ☐ |
| ☐ |
| ☐ |

# July/August

**26** SUNDAY

**27** MONDAY

**28** TUESDAY

**29** WEDNESDAY

**30** THURSDAY

# 2020

**31 FRIDAY**

**1 SATURDAY**

| | TO DO |
|---|---|
| ☐ | |
| ☐ | |
| ☐ | |
| ☐ | |
| ☐ | |
| ☐ | |
| ☐ | |
| ☐ | |
| ☐ | |
| ☐ | |
| ☐ | |
| ☐ | |
| ☐ | |
| ☐ | |
| ☐ | |
| ☐ | |
| ☐ | |
| ☐ | |

# August

**2 SUNDAY**

**3 MONDAY**

**4 TUESDAY**

**5 WEDNESDAY**

**6 THURSDAY**

# 2020

7     FRIDAY

8     SATURDAY

## TO DO

- [ ]
- [ ]
- [ ]
- [ ]
- [ ]
- [ ]
- [ ]
- [ ]
- [ ]
- [ ]
- [ ]
- [ ]
- [ ]
- [ ]
- [ ]
- [ ]
- [ ]

# August

9    SUNDAY

10    MONDAY

11    TUESDAY

12    WEDNESDAY

13    THURSDAY

# 2020

**14  FRIDAY**

**15  SATURDAY**

| TO DO |
|---|
| ☐ |
| ☐ |
| ☐ |
| ☐ |
| ☐ |
| ☐ |
| ☐ |
| ☐ |
| ☐ |
| ☐ |
| ☐ |
| ☐ |
| ☐ |
| ☐ |
| ☐ |
| ☐ |
| ☐ |

# August

**16** SUNDAY

**17** MONDAY

**18** TUESDAY

**19** WEDNESDAY

**20** THURSDAY

# 2020

**21 FRIDAY**

**22 SATURDAY**

| TO DO |
|---|
| ☐ |
| ☐ |
| ☐ |
| ☐ |
| ☐ |
| ☐ |
| ☐ |
| ☐ |
| ☐ |
| ☐ |
| ☐ |
| ☐ |
| ☐ |
| ☐ |
| ☐ |
| ☐ |
| ☐ |

# August

**23** SUNDAY

**24** MONDAY

**25** TUESDAY

**26** WEDNESDAY

**27** THURSDAY

# 2020

**28 FRIDAY**

**29 SATURDAY**

| TO DO |
|---|
| ☐ |
| ☐ |
| ☐ |
| ☐ |
| ☐ |
| ☐ |
| ☐ |
| ☐ |
| ☐ |
| ☐ |
| ☐ |
| ☐ |
| ☐ |
| ☐ |
| ☐ |
| ☐ |
| ☐ |

# August/September

**30** SUNDAY

**31** MONDAY

**1** TUESDAY

**2** WEDNESDAY

**3** THURSDAY

# 2020

**4   FRIDAY**

**5   SATURDAY**

| TO DO |
|---|
| ☐ |
| ☐ |
| ☐ |
| ☐ |
| ☐ |
| ☐ |
| ☐ |
| ☐ |
| ☐ |
| ☐ |
| ☐ |
| ☐ |
| ☐ |
| ☐ |
| ☐ |
| ☐ |
| ☐ |

# September

**6** SUNDAY

**7** MONDAY

**8** TUESDAY

**9** WEDNESDAY

**10** THURSDAY

# 2020

**11 FRIDAY**

**12 SATURDAY**

| TO DO |
|---|
| ☐ |
| ☐ |
| ☐ |
| ☐ |
| ☐ |
| ☐ |
| ☐ |
| ☐ |
| ☐ |
| ☐ |
| ☐ |
| ☐ |
| ☐ |
| ☐ |
| ☐ |
| ☐ |
| ☐ |

# September

**13** SUNDAY

**14** MONDAY

**15** TUESDAY

**16** WEDNESDAY

**17** THURSDAY

# 2020

**18 FRIDAY**

**19 SATURDAY**

## TO DO

- [ ]
- [ ]
- [ ]
- [ ]
- [ ]
- [ ]
- [ ]
- [ ]
- [ ]
- [ ]
- [ ]
- [ ]
- [ ]
- [ ]
- [ ]
- [ ]
- [ ]

# September

**20** SUNDAY

**21** MONDAY

**22** TUESDAY

**23** WEDNESDAY

**24** THURSDAY

# 2020

**25  FRIDAY**

**26  SATURDAY**

| TO DO |
|---|
| ☐ |
| ☐ |
| ☐ |
| ☐ |
| ☐ |
| ☐ |
| ☐ |
| ☐ |
| ☐ |
| ☐ |
| ☐ |
| ☐ |
| ☐ |
| ☐ |
| ☐ |
| ☐ |
| ☐ |

# September/October

**27** SUNDAY

**28** MONDAY

**29** TUESDAY

**30** WEDNESDAY

**1** THURSDAY

# 2020

**2  FRIDAY**

**3  SATURDAY**

| | TO DO |
|---|---|
| ☐ | |
| ☐ | |
| ☐ | |
| ☐ | |
| ☐ | |
| ☐ | |
| ☐ | |
| ☐ | |
| ☐ | |
| ☐ | |
| ☐ | |
| ☐ | |
| ☐ | |
| ☐ | |
| ☐ | |
| ☐ | |
| ☐ | |
| ☐ | |

# October

**4 SUNDAY**

**5 MONDAY**

**6 TUESDAY**

**7 WEDNESDAY**

**8 THURSDAY**

# 2020

9    FRIDAY

10    SATURDAY

| TO DO |
|---|
| ☐ |
| ☐ |
| ☐ |
| ☐ |
| ☐ |
| ☐ |
| ☐ |
| ☐ |
| ☐ |
| ☐ |
| ☐ |
| ☐ |
| ☐ |
| ☐ |
| ☐ |
| ☐ |
| ☐ |

# October

**11** SUNDAY

**12** MONDAY

**13** TUESDAY

**14** WEDNESDAY

**15** THURSDAY

# 2020

**16 FRIDAY**

**17 SATURDAY**

| TO DO |
|---|
| ☐ |
| ☐ |
| ☐ |
| ☐ |
| ☐ |
| ☐ |
| ☐ |
| ☐ |
| ☐ |
| ☐ |
| ☐ |
| ☐ |
| ☐ |
| ☐ |
| ☐ |
| ☐ |
| ☐ |

# October

**18** SUNDAY

**19** MONDAY

**20** TUESDAY

**21** WEDNESDAY

**22** THURSDAY

# 2020

**23  FRIDAY**

**24  SATURDAY**

| | TO DO |
|---|---|
| | ☐ |
| | ☐ |
| | ☐ |
| | ☐ |
| | ☐ |
| | ☐ |
| | ☐ |
| | ☐ |
| | ☐ |
| | ☐ |
| | ☐ |
| | ☐ |
| | ☐ |
| | ☐ |
| | ☐ |
| | ☐ |
| | ☐ |
| | ☐ |

# October

**25** SUNDAY

**26** MONDAY

**27** TUESDAY

**28** WEDNESDAY

**29** THURSDAY

# 2020

30   FRIDAY

31   SATURDAY

| | TO DO |
|---|---|
| | ☐ |
| | ☐ |
| | ☐ |
| | ☐ |
| | ☐ |
| | ☐ |
| | ☐ |
| | ☐ |
| | ☐ |
| | ☐ |
| | ☐ |
| | ☐ |
| | ☐ |
| | ☐ |
| | ☐ |
| | ☐ |
| | ☐ |

# November

**1 SUNDAY**

**2 MONDAY**

**3 TUESDAY**

**4 WEDNESDAY**

**5 THURSDAY**

# 2020

6     FRIDAY

7     SATURDAY

## TO DO

- [ ]
- [ ]
- [ ]
- [ ]
- [ ]
- [ ]
- [ ]
- [ ]
- [ ]
- [ ]
- [ ]
- [ ]
- [ ]
- [ ]
- [ ]
- [ ]
- [ ]

# November

**8** SUNDAY

**9** MONDAY

**10** TUESDAY

**11** WEDNESDAY

**12** THURSDAY

# 2020

**13 FRIDAY**

**14 SATURDAY**

| TO DO |
|---|
| ☐ |
| ☐ |
| ☐ |
| ☐ |
| ☐ |
| ☐ |
| ☐ |
| ☐ |
| ☐ |
| ☐ |
| ☐ |
| ☐ |
| ☐ |
| ☐ |
| ☐ |
| ☐ |
| ☐ |
| ☐ |

# November

**15** SUNDAY

**16** MONDAY

**17** TUESDAY

**18** WEDNESDAY

**19** THURSDAY

# 2020

**20  FRIDAY**

**21  SATURDAY**

|  | TO DO |
|---|---|
| ☐ | |
| ☐ | |
| ☐ | |
| ☐ | |
| ☐ | |
| ☐ | |
| ☐ | |
| ☐ | |
| ☐ | |
| ☐ | |
| ☐ | |
| ☐ | |
| ☐ | |
| ☐ | |
| ☐ | |
| ☐ | |
| ☐ | |

# November

**22 SUNDAY**

**23 MONDAY**

**24 TUESDAY**

**25 WEDNESDAY**

**26 THURSDAY**

# 2020

**27 FRIDAY**

**28 SATURDAY**

| TO DO |
|---|
| ☐ |
| ☐ |
| ☐ |
| ☐ |
| ☐ |
| ☐ |
| ☐ |
| ☐ |
| ☐ |
| ☐ |
| ☐ |
| ☐ |
| ☐ |
| ☐ |
| ☐ |
| ☐ |
| ☐ |

# November/December

**29 SUNDAY**

**30 MONDAY**

**1 TUESDAY**

**2 WEDNESDAY**

**3 THURSDAY**

# 2020

4    FRIDAY

5    SATURDAY

## TO DO

- [ ]
- [ ]
- [ ]
- [ ]
- [ ]
- [ ]
- [ ]
- [ ]
- [ ]
- [ ]
- [ ]
- [ ]
- [ ]
- [ ]
- [ ]
- [ ]
- [ ]

# December

**6** SUNDAY

**7** MONDAY

**8** TUESDAY

**9** WEDNESDAY

**10** THURSDAY

# 2020

**11  FRIDAY**

**12  SATURDAY**

| TO DO |
|---|
| ☐ |
| ☐ |
| ☐ |
| ☐ |
| ☐ |
| ☐ |
| ☐ |
| ☐ |
| ☐ |
| ☐ |
| ☐ |
| ☐ |
| ☐ |
| ☐ |
| ☐ |
| ☐ |
| ☐ |
| ☐ |

# December

**13 SUNDAY**

**14 MONDAY**

**15 TUESDAY**

**16 WEDNESDAY**

**17 THURSDAY**

# 2020

**18 FRIDAY**

**19 SATURDAY**

| TO DO |
|---|
| ☐ |
| ☐ |
| ☐ |
| ☐ |
| ☐ |
| ☐ |
| ☐ |
| ☐ |
| ☐ |
| ☐ |
| ☐ |
| ☐ |
| ☐ |
| ☐ |
| ☐ |
| ☐ |
| ☐ |

# December

**20** SUNDAY

**21** MONDAY

**22** TUESDAY

**23** WEDNESDAY

**24** THURSDAY

# 2020

**25  FRIDAY**

**26  SATURDAY**

| TO DO |
|---|
| ☐ |
| ☐ |
| ☐ |
| ☐ |
| ☐ |
| ☐ |
| ☐ |
| ☐ |
| ☐ |
| ☐ |
| ☐ |
| ☐ |
| ☐ |
| ☐ |
| ☐ |
| ☐ |
| ☐ |
| ☐ |

# December

**27** SUNDAY

**28** MONDAY

**29** TUESDAY

**30** WEDNESDAY

**31** THURSDAY

# 2020

1 FRIDAY

2 SATURDAY

| TO DO |
|---|
| ☐ |
| ☐ |
| ☐ |
| ☐ |
| ☐ |
| ☐ |
| ☐ |
| ☐ |
| ☐ |
| ☐ |
| ☐ |
| ☐ |
| ☐ |
| ☐ |
| ☐ |
| ☐ |
| ☐ |

# NOTES

# NOTES

# NOTES

NOTES

CPSIA information can be obtained
at www.ICGtesting.com
Printed in the USA
LVHW06063229101
635550LV00005B/678/P